# Red-Tails in Manhattan
## The Story of Pale Male

Heera Kang

## Contents

Rigby
A Harcourt Achieve Imprint

www.Rigby.com
1-800-531-5015

# Stranded

Imagine that your car breaks down during a trip across the country. There is no sign of anything for miles in any direction. There are no houses, supermarkets, hospitals, or other buildings anywhere around.

You don't see any people, yet you know you are not alone. A deer streaks across the road, eyeing you cautiously. Mountain rabbits and other small rodents scurry around your feet. Imagine you had to survive in this unfamiliar place for days, maybe longer. What are your first concerns—food, shelter, or safety from what you sense hides in the shadows?

You have just put yourself in the place of Pale Male, a remarkable red-tailed hawk who has adapted to life in an environment that is very unfamiliar to him.

The red-tail hawk called Pale Male is a rare bird indeed. He made his home in the hustle and bustle of New York City, rather than out in nature.

Red-tailed hawks live in forests, prairies, grasslands, and sometimes deserts. And even though these winged creatures are found in many different areas of the country, it was a big surprise when a young, light-colored red-tail decided to make his home in the heart of New York City on the island of Manhattan.

How would Pale Male survive? What would he eat? Could he raise a family there?

Pale Male's story is best told through the eyes of someone who often visits Central Park. Over the years, people of all ages have fallen in love with this fascinating creature. Let's follow along with one of these admirers and watch Pale Male take Manhattan!

# CHAPTER ONE

# Home, Sweet Home?

New York City has the highest population of any city in the United States. It takes pride in its huge skyscrapers, not in trees or wildlife. So why would a hawk choose to live among the sidewalks and streets?

Buried within this busy city lies a man-made getaway called Central Park. Here you'll find 843 acres of rolling hills and meadows, tall trees, and sparkling lakes. Central Park was meant to be a fun and relaxing place for humans to go, but it's also home to birds, small animals, and insects. From a hawk's point of view, Central Park looks very promising.

## NOVEMBER 3, 1991

What luck! Today, while I was hanging out by the pond, I caught a glimpse of a red-tailed hawk that I think was flying south for the winter.

All kinds of birds fly over Central Park on their way south to warmer weather, and many stop in for a snack or maybe a bath in the pond. I've seen lots of sparrows and blue jays, and even some neat-looking woodpeckers, but seeing this hawk was a real treat! He was clearly a red-tail hawk because of the red feathers on his tail, but also because of the light coloring on his chest and the darker feathers on his back. It was amazing to see how easily the hawk glided across the sky. Just a few flaps of those powerful wings, and he rode the gusts of wind up into the sky.

## DECEMBER 17, 1991

A layer of snow covered Central Park all morning, dusting the trees with flakes. I was surprised to see the hawk I'd spotted back in November was still in the city, sitting on a branch and looking down into the park. Parts of him were as light as the snow on the leaves. His head turned from side to side, slow and controlled. He watched the ground for his next meal. I held my breath, waiting to see what would happen next.

In the next instant, he was off. He swooped down with perfect aim to snatch up a squirrel. The squirrel didn't know what hit it. This was my first time seeing a hawk have a meal—it wasn't easy to watch. If the squirrel wasn't dead when it got snatched up, it certainly was by the time the hawk landed back on his perch.

Central Park was designed to be a quiet place for people and animals to enjoy. If this hawk stays, he'll be the first one to make a home here.

## MARCH 26, 1992

The light-colored hawk I saw during the winter never left Central Park! I wonder if he'll really try to make a home here. It'll be amazing if he does.

People have started calling him Pale Male, and he's not alone anymore. We were all surprised to see another red-tail gliding above the trees. This hawk was clearly larger than Pale Male, which means that she's a female. The female red-tails are always bigger than the males. I wonder why that is.

## MARCH 27, 1992

Today I saw the female sitting on the ledge of a building just outside the park. Before long, I spotted Pale Male riding a gust of wind toward her. He was carrying a dead pigeon—at least I think it was dead. I guess it was a present for her, or something to convince her to stay.

The present worked! The two of them flew around together all afternoon. Pale Male swooped away in a big loop and then flew back to her, only to swoop away again. It's clearly a courtship dance between new mates.

A lot of people are starting to get interested in Pale Male. Now that he has a partner, I think he may stay here for a while.

# EYE ON RED-TAILS

Before we go any further, let's learn a little more about what kind of bird Pale Male is. Check out the different parts of the red-tail hawk, then take a guess about whether Pale Male will be able to survive in the big city!

Hawks need to have very sharp eyes to see their prey from high above ground. For this reason red-tails can see 8 to 10 times better than humans see. They even have an extra eyelid that closes from side to side, wiping moisture from their eyes.

When red-tails dive after prey, they can fly as fast as 120 miles per hour! Have you ever opened the window of a moving car and had the wind hit you in the face? It makes it hard to breathe, doesn't it? Hawks are able to close their nostrils to block out the wind while flying at high speeds.

Red-tails hunt and eat mostly small prey, but they don't have teeth like humans and other animals. They have sharp, hooked beaks that are perfectly formed for tearing into their dinner!

Red-tail hawks have long, rounded wings that allow them to soar and hover as they keep a lookout for their next meal.

Red-tailed hawks are dark on top and light underneath, with a reddish tail. Squirrels, mice, and other prey move quickly, so hawks need to be able to sneak up on them without being noticed. If you look up at a red-tail flying above, its light underside helps it blend in with the sky.

A hawk's tail feathers work much like a boat's sail. When fanned out, the tail feathers help the hawk move in different directions. When folded in, the hawk can glide at higher speeds.

The red-tail's claws are called talons. Talons are sharp and strong, just like a beak. It would be a waste to spend all of that energy tracking and swooping down on prey only to drop it because of weak talons.

# CHAPTER TWO

# Pale Male
# and First Love

As strange as New York City might seem to a red-tail, things were working out pretty well for Pale Male. There were plenty of high places for him to use when watching out for food and enemies. Plus, Central Park was filled with tasty critters.

After the male hawk has established his territory, he's ready for a mate. In the wild, he would make loud calls and dance around in the sky to attract females. But what female hawk would be able to hear a male's call above the horns and sirens of New York City?

Nevertheless, a female red-tail did answer Pale Male's calls. She was given the romantic name *First Love*. Together, Pale Male and First Love were ready to take the next step— house hunting.

## MARCH 13, 1993

I still wonder why red-tail females are usually 25 percent larger than males. It seems like males should be larger because they do most of the hunting and protect the nest from attacks.

Maybe the females need to be larger so that they can cover the eggs in the nest. Or, they might be larger so that they can protect the nest while the males are away.

I'll have to research this some more.

## Height Comparison of Red-tail Hawks

The average female is 26 inches.

The average male is 22 inches.

Height in Inches

26
24
22
20
18
16
14
12
10
8
6
4
2

## MARCH 15, 1993

It's still pretty cold outside, but it's not so bad that I couldn't spend some time catching up with Pale Male. He's got First Love now, so I know they're going to start building a nest soon. Hawks don't like other animals to know where they build their homes. If they sense that their nest is being watched, they might leave it altogether and start over somewhere else.

From what I've read, red-tailed hawks build their nests in places that they can fly away from easily in case of danger. They also like to have a good view of the surrounding area below.

## MARCH 18, 1993

Maybe these birds know something I don't. Today Pale Male and First Love were carrying twigs to a tree near a baseball diamond. The diamond is in the Great Lawn—a popular place with lots of activities going on all the time. Maybe they've gotten used to humans, but I still think making a nest so close to all of those people can't be a good idea.

## MARCH 19, 1993

Well, it didn't work out. Their nest wasn't strong enough. It broke up and fell out of the tree. The sad thing is that someone found a broken hawk egg near the baseball diamond.

Twig by twig, Pale Male worked tirelessly to bring materials to build a nest. But did he choose the best place to build a home?

## APRIL 30, 1993

Today I got really close to Pale Male's new nest. This new location is just as crowded as the baseball diamond was, and it's very close to the Summer Stage, which gets really loud with music concerts and other things. And something tells me the red-tails aren't here for the music.

I have a bad feeling about this. Some people also think Pale Male and First Love are too close to where crows nest. I've heard that crows can be very territorial. They don't like other birds to get in their way.

## MAY 1, 1993

Something horrible has happened! First Love was attacked by crows! They were flying around her in all directions, trying to get her to run into something. It was terrible! She flew into the side of a building, then fell to the ground!

Then the crows went after Pale Male. He was trying to find a way to break free, but there were too many of them. Poor Pale Male hit the side of a building, too!

## MAY 10, 1993

After more than a week, Pale Male has returned to Central Park. He wasn't too badly hurt when he hit that building. First Love, on the other hand, was not so lucky. The New York Audubon Society, a bird and wildlife rescue group, sent her to hawk experts who could help.

Red-tailed hawks usually stay with one mate for their whole lives, unless something separates them. Pale Male, within a year of living in New York City, was left without a mate. I think it's about time a stroke of good luck came his way.

Crows will attack in a way that's called "mobbing." In large groups, they'll swarm and swoop around their target to confuse it and make it crash into something.

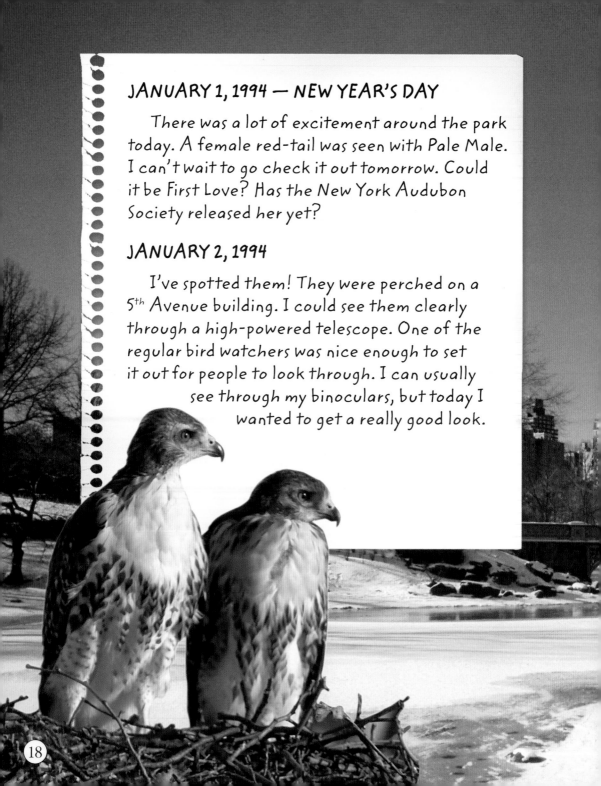

## JANUARY 1, 1994 — NEW YEAR'S DAY

There was a lot of excitement around the park today. A female red-tail was seen with Pale Male. I can't wait to go check it out tomorrow. Could it be First Love? Has the New York Audubon Society released her yet?

## JANUARY 2, 1994

I've spotted them! They were perched on a 5th Avenue building. I could see them clearly through a high-powered telescope. One of the regular bird watchers was nice enough to set it out for people to look through. I can usually see through my binoculars, but today I wanted to get a really good look.

The first thing I noticed was that this female's head seemed darker than First Love's. That can happen sometimes when birds molt, which is when old feathers fall out and new ones grow in. This new female is large, just like First Love, but I don't think it's her. Could there be a new woman in Pale Male's life?

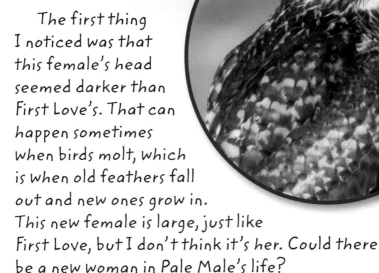

## JANUARY 4, 1994

I read today that after First Love recovered from the crow attack, the hawk experts who took care of her put a band around her ankle and set her free. They'll use the numbers on the band like an identification bracelet, so that they can watch her and see how she's doing.

Well, there's no band on Pale Male's new female. People are starting to call this new hawk Chocolate. Even though I wish it was First Love, I'm glad Pale Male found another mate.

## MARCH 6, 1994

It's been two months since Chocolate came around, and things are looking much better for Pale Male. It's a struggle being a pioneer, and New York is a tough town. In his early attempts at nesting, Pale Male did what most hawks would have done— he built a nest on the highest tree he could find near food. How could he have known he was getting into crow territory?

Making the best of a difficult situation, Pale Male builds a nest high on an apartment on 5th Avenue. He uses twigs and other materials the city provides, including a piece of kitchen flooring.

## MARCH 7, 1994

This afternoon was warm and sunny, making it perfect bird-watching weather. I saw Pale Male carrying a twig, which meant only one thing. He was trying to make another nest!

I was curious about which part of Central Park he'd chosen, but instead he flew out of the park and across 5th Avenue. He landed on the 12th floor of a really nice apartment building.

There he was, perched on the ledge of that fancy building with all of these spiky nails around him. People use those spikes to keep pigeons from sitting on the buildings. It's called *anti-pigeon wire*.

It sure didn't bother Pale Male much. He just built his nest around the wire.

## MARCH 8, 1994

Wow! I knew this was a smart hawk! The anti-pigeon wire is helping to keep the nest in place. It can get really windy and stormy in New York City, especially up there on the 12th floor. Some people are joking that he has the best view in town. I've heard that apartments in that building can cost 10 to 15 million dollars! Pale Male sure has expensive taste.

# CHANGE OF ADDRESS

You can definitely teach a hawk new tricks. Pale Male has come a long way since gathering twigs around a baseball diamond. Let's look at the lessons he's learned as he set out to build a nest in the city.

The **FIRST** nest near the baseball diamond in the Great Lawn wasn't nearly strong enough. It was also dangerously close to crowds of people.

Little did Pale Male know, but he built his **SECOND** nest right in the middle of crow territory.

To get away from crows and other enemies in the park, Pale Male and Chocolate move across the street to a 5th Avenue high-rise. They couldn't have chosen a better spot than on the 12th floor of this apartment building. The anti-pigeon wire is perfect for holding the nest down when winds blow.

In addition, they're well out of crow territory but still have a perfect view over their hunting ground in Central Park. And they've chosen the side of the building facing southwest. This side shields them from bad weather.

This nest is the **WINNER!**

# CHAPTER THREE

# Waiting for Chicks

Red-tails usually only keep nests when they have eggs, but if the nest holds, they'll come back the next year to use it again. The 12th floor was the perfect spot for Pale Male's nest. It had a great view of his hunting ground in Central Park, there were no crows in sight, and it was kept in place by anti-pigeon wire.

With the nest all ready to go, Pale Male and Chocolate were ready for a family. But as it turned out, they weren't having much luck starting one. Red-tails will usually start incubating, or sitting on their eggs to keep them warm, in mid-spring. This lasts for around 28 days until the eggs hatch. The female sits on the eggs most of the time while the male hunts for food.

In 1995, spring came and no eggs were laid. April was fast approaching, and the time for incubating had almost come and gone. All of New York City was rooting for Pale Male and Chocolate, but it turned out to be a disappointing spring. No eggs would be seen until the following year.

The regular hawk watchers at the pond have been waiting anxiously for chicks. They know that if the red-tails can't raise chicks here, they'll leave.

# MAP TO CENTRAL PARK

Let's take a moment to think about how Pale Male ended up in Central Park. Red-tails in North America will fly south in the fall in order to get to warmer weather during the winter. Take a look at the map below to see the path that might have brought Pale Male to Central Park. Then check the map of Central Park and see if you can find the places you've read about so far.

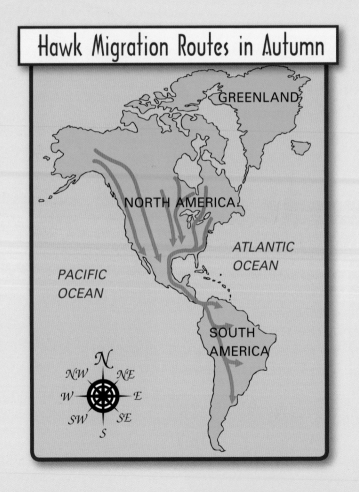

## Hawk Migration Routes in Autumn

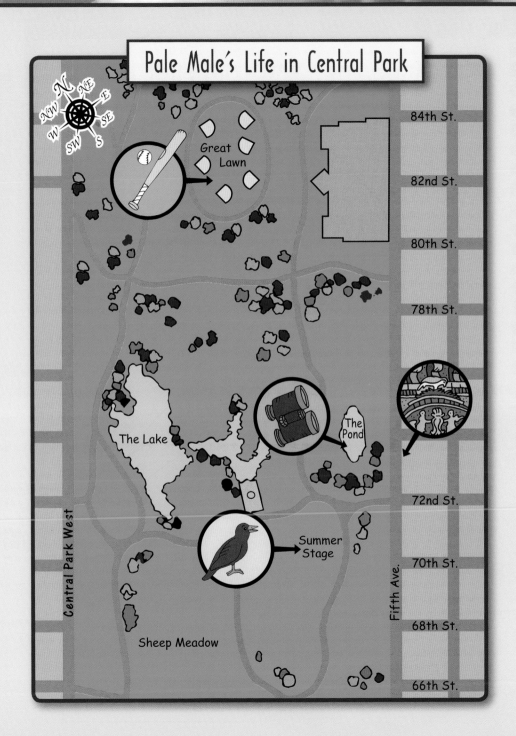

# Pale Male's Life in Central Park

## FEBRUARY 14, 1996 — VALENTINE'S DAY

We're all a little confused. It's starting to get more difficult keeping track of Pale Male's love life! He's now together with a female who wears an ankle band. Could this be First Love, and she's found her way back to him?

Or is it Chocolate? We haven't seen her around for a while. Maybe she got hurt, and the experts from the Audubon Society put an ankle band on her, just like they did for First Love. Or, this could be a new female altogether. It's a mystery.

Whoever the new female is, we're calling her Mom because there are three eggs in Pale Male's nest!

Pale Male definitely wants to be a good father. He's been seen sitting on his eggs, helping to keep the little ones warm and safe.

## FEBRUARY 25, 1996

After the red-tail's eggs are laid, it's typically the job of the female to do the sitting and keep the eggs warm. The male usually brings her food to keep her plump and happy. He also keeps his family safe until the eggs hatch.

This means Pale Male and Mom are having to work as a team. One of them sits on the eggs at all times. It's usually Mom, but I've seen Pale Male doing his share of egg-sitting. He looks like a proud father to me.

I've read that red-tails will lay two or three eggs each year. The chicks grow inside the egg for about a month, then they start pecking from inside of the egg until they are free of the shell. That could take a day or two.

I guess we won't see anything until the end of March.

## MARCH 30, 1996

I went down to the park today because the trees and flowers were blossoming all over the place. I thought that it would be a perfect day to welcome the chicks.

I looked up into the nest with my binoculars. Could it be? Pale Male brought some food to the nest, and it looked like he was tearing it up into little bits.

Then I saw the furry little heads of three chicks! They looked fluffy and soft, like they were covered in cotton balls. Their beaks were open, chirping for food.

It was so exciting watching Pale Male and Mom take care of the chicks. Just as they did with the eggs, one of them stays in the nest while the other hunts for food. I can see by her beak and talons that Mom is a great hunter!

## APRIL 28, 1996

Just last month those fuzzy little chicks could barely waddle around. Now they have light-colored feathers, and they're moving around the nest a lot. Some people say they'll be learning to fly soon. I can't believe those little guys could possibly be ready to fly to the park from the 12$^{th}$ floor. There is nothing in-between except cars and street! They can't possibly be ready.

## MAY 10, 1996

Pale Male must think the chicks are ready to fly. A little while ago, I saw him holding out a piece of food to coax the babies out of the nest.

Chicks who have grown their feathers used for flying are called fledglings, and Pale Male's fledglings are getting very excited about learning to fly. One of them was really flapping its wings. There was fluff flying everywhere!

It's such a long way down, though, and what if one flies into the pond? I'll stick around for a while longer to see what happens.

## May 11, 1996

I stuck around long enough yesterday to see one of the fledglings make the jump out of the nest. He stumbled a bit at first, but soon he was soaring through the sky.

Then the second fledgling took the leap. This one flew straight into Central Park. I think he bothered some blue jays because the jays started diving at his head! I noticed Pale Male watching from a distance. If the fledgling were in real trouble, I knew he'd have come to the rescue.

## MAY 12, 1996

It's two days after the first flight, and now all three fledglings are flyers! It took some coaxing to get the third one out of the nest. His parents and siblings had to fly around the nest to cheer him on. Soon he was up in the air, soaring like a proud hawk.

Great flying lesson, Pale Male. Now it's time to teach your kids to hunt.

Fledgling hawks stay in the nest for about 45 days, until they've grown the feathers they'll need for flight.

# FLEDGLINGS IN FLIGHT SCHOOL

## So what do we know?

- Young red-tails that are learning to fly are called fledglings.
- About one month after they've broken out of their shells, the chicks start moving around a lot more in the nest. This means they're ready for flight school.
- Fledglings that are afraid to leave the nest are coaxed out by the parents holding out bits of food for them.

Red-tail fledglings usually have a short distance to fly out of the nest. They start small by hopping from branch to branch until they are strong enough to fly freely.

What do you suppose Pale Male's fledglings are going to do? There are no branches on the 5th Avenue high-rise, and it's 1,500 feet to the nearest tree. It seems as though Pale Male's ideal nest location is turning into a nightmare for the three little fledglings!

But as we've seen, red-tail hawks are able to adapt to tough challenges and difficult environments, and Pale Male's chicks really take after their father.

When you can't learn to fly from branch to branch, you go from building to building! The fledgling flyers go from ledge to ledge until they are strong enough to soar for longer distances.

What smart hawks!

Usually, young fledglings can hop from branch to branch, then to the ground. Pale Male's fledglings have to fly 1,500 feet over busy traffic just to get to a tree.

# CHAPTER FOUR

# You Never Forget Your First Love

## MARCH 15, 1997

Another year has passed, and it's spring again in Central Park. Pale Male has made New York City his permanent home. He's the first red-tailed hawk to successfully nest on the ledge of a building in the city. Other kinds of hawks have been known to nest on buildings, but never red-tails.

I'm excited about another season of eggs and chicks and flight school. Both Pale Male and Mom have been busy with the same nest they used to raise their first fledglings. Everything has to be perfect when Mom lays her new eggs.

There is supposed to be a big surprise down at the pond later today. Someone is bringing a really powerful telescope to the park. We're determined to read the numbers on Mom's ankle band. Those of us who have been with Pale Male from the beginning need to know—who exactly is this female red-tail we've been calling Mom?

Instinct brought First Love back to Central Park. She and Pale Male finally have the family they wanted all those years ago.

## MARCH 16, 1997

I can't believe it! Today we got to read the numbers on Mom's ankle band. They match First Love's! It's her!

My mind is racing to think of exactly when First Love came back to Central Park. After the crow attack, she was taken to an expert for help. The expert let her free in a wildlife refuge in New Jersey. That's more than forty miles away!

## MAY 25, 1997

I spent the day today watching Pale Male and First Love with their three new chicks. I've decided that it doesn't matter exactly when First Love made it back to Central Park or how she found her way from the wildlife refuge. All I can say is that these red-tails are truly amazing.

I'm looking forward to many warm summer days watching these remarkable creatures.

## OCTOBER 13, 1997

Today I went down to the park as usual. Everyone was being very quiet. I got really worried. Finally someone told me what had happened.

First Love was found dead on the ledge of a museum. She'd eaten a pigeon that must have been poisoned. Some people can't stand all of the pigeons we have in the city. They put out poisoned food for the pigeons to eat.

Will Pale Male be able to make it without her? Red-tail hawks usually choose one mate for life. First Love was proof of this when she made her way back to Pale Male after the crow attack. But it's clear that the red-tails on 5$^{th}$ Avenue have more than crows to be afraid of in the big city.

The red-tails have to watch out for humans as well.

# THE HUMAN FACTOR

We've seen how the red-tails have survived in New York City, but now let's turn our attention to the other animals in Pale Male's ecosystem. An ecosystem describes the way plants and animals live together as a unit within a particular environment, such as New York City. Sometimes the animals live together peacefully. Sometimes they don't.

We already know about Pale Male's enemies—mainly the crows. Then there's his prey, which are the critters in Central Park. But what about the people? We can't ignore the role that humans play in the ecosystem these red-tails must live in.

There are two different views people have of Pale Male living in the city. Many people enjoy having him around. Pale Male's admirers down at the pond have helped him along the way. They have joined together to make sure his nest is safe and that he always has a home in New York City.

On the other hand, his presence also causes some problems for the residents of Pale Male's apartment building. Pale Male leaves bird droppings and dead animal pieces out on the ledge. This can get smelly and annoying when you have to clean it up.

As you can see, humans can be both good and bad for the red-tails. When the crows injured First Love and Pale Male, humans nursed them back to health. However, a poisoned pigeon possibly caused First Love's death.

The balance in an ecosystem is not always stable.

# CHAPTER FIVE

# From Fledgling to Father

## MARCH 9, 1998

After we lost First Love last fall, some wonder if the red-tails could keep living on 5<sup>th</sup> Avenue.

One way to tell whether an animal will continue to survive in a new place is to watch its children. That's why I'm excited about this new hawk we've all been keeping our eye on.

Last year a young red-tail that looks a lot like Pale Male tried to start a family of his own. We're calling him *Pale Male, Jr.*

Pale Male, Jr. got off to a rough start. His nest was totally blown away by strong winds, and there were eggs in the nest! What's more, his mate flew into falcon territory. They attacked and killed her in the air. These are the same kinds of troubles Pale Male suffered through. Will Pale Male, Jr. learn how to survive in the city?

## MARCH 18, 1998

I've spotted Pale Male, Jr.! His nest is on another expensive apartment building—the Trump Parc on Central Park South and 6$^{th}$ Avenue. The nest is so high up, it makes Pale Male's nest look safe. It might be a dangerous nest site, but so far things are going well. He even has one chick!

Pale Male is now a grandfather!

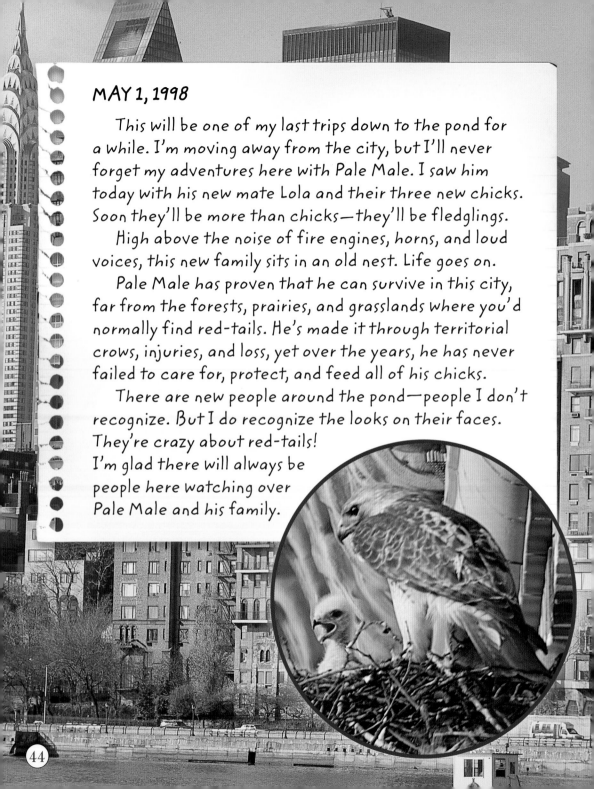

## MAY 1, 1998

This will be one of my last trips down to the pond for a while. I'm moving away from the city, but I'll never forget my adventures here with Pale Male. I saw him today with his new mate Lola and their three new chicks. Soon they'll be more than chicks—they'll be fledglings.

High above the noise of fire engines, horns, and loud voices, this new family sits in an old nest. Life goes on.

Pale Male has proven that he can survive in this city, far from the forests, prairies, and grasslands where you'd normally find red-tails. He's made it through territorial crows, injuries, and loss, yet over the years, he has never failed to care for, protect, and feed all of his chicks.

There are new people around the pond—people I don't recognize. But I do recognize the looks on their faces. They're crazy about red-tails! I'm glad there will always be people here watching over Pale Male and his family.

# These Days

Today, some people in Pale Male's apartment building still want him gone. And the people at the pond are still fighting to keep him where he is. The nest on 5th Avenue is safe for now, but it looks like Pale Male will always need the help and watchful eye of his friends.

# UNNATURAL BEAUTY

In an ecosystem, two different kinds of animals sometimes come to depend on one another. They need each other for things like food, shelter, and safety. This relationship can benefit just one animal, or both can benefit.

Pale Male will never know that the people watching him from the pond helped save his nest many times. They gave the hawks medical attention after the crow attack. And many are fighting to stop pigeon poisoning.

What do the people of New York City get out of this relationship? Pale Male, First Love, and the other red-tails are things of "unnatural beauty," just like Central Park itself.

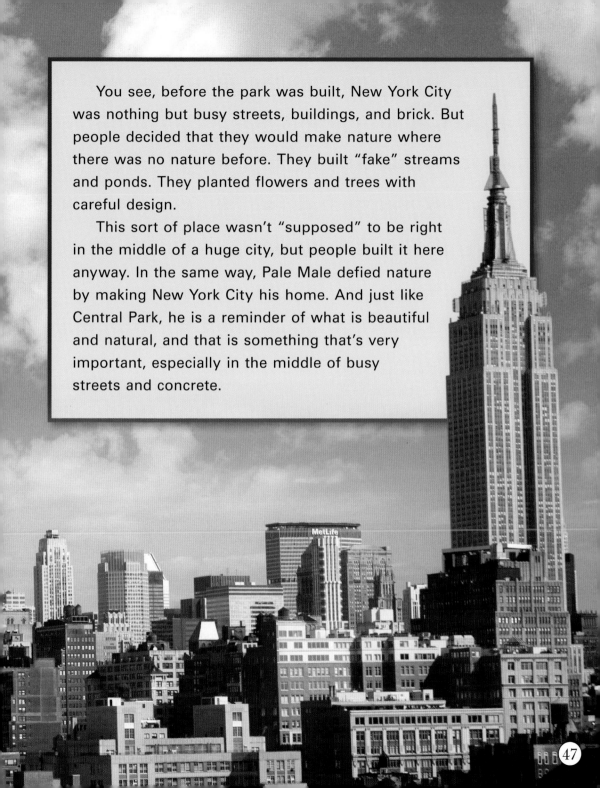

You see, before the park was built, New York City was nothing but busy streets, buildings, and brick. But people decided that they would make nature where there was no nature before. They built "fake" streams and ponds. They planted flowers and trees with careful design.

This sort of place wasn't "supposed" to be right in the middle of a huge city, but people built it here anyway. In the same way, Pale Male defied nature by making New York City his home. And just like Central Park, he is a reminder of what is beautiful and natural, and that is something that's very important, especially in the middle of busy streets and concrete.

# Index